Tom Wolfe Carves

Old-World Santas

Photography by and text written with Molly Higgins

Schiffer Publishing Ltd

4880 Lower Valley Road, Atglen, PA 19310 USA

Contents

Published by Schiffer Publishing Ltd.
4880 Lower Valley Road
Atglen, PA 19310
Phone: (610) 593-1777; Fax: (610) 593-2002
E-mail: Schifferbk@aol.com
Please visit our web site catalog at www.schifferbooks.com or write for a free catalog.

We are always looking for authors to write books on new and related subjects. If you have an idea
for a book, please contact us at the above address.

This book may be purchased from the publisher.
Please include $3.95 for shipping.

In Europe, Schiffer books are distributed by
Bushwood Books
6 Marksbury Ave.
Kew Gardens
Surrey TW9 4JF England
Phone: 44 (0)20-8392-8585; Fax: 44 (0)20-8392-9876
E-mail: Bushwd@aol.com
Free postage in the UK. Europe: Air mail at cost.
Please try your bookstore first.

Copyright © 2001 by Tom Wolfe
Library of Congress Card Number: 2001086979

Designed by John P. Cheek
Type set in University Roman BT/Souvenir Lt BT
ISBN: 0-7643-1351-7
Printed in China

Introduction

Few things capture the charm of Christmas like the old-world Santa Claus. You might also know him as St. Nicholas or Father Christmas. He shines with the magic and tradition of the holiday spirit as he marches on to deliver toys to each boy and girl on his list. He is humble, and he is wise, but he has a sparkle in his eye that shows what a merry elf he really is.

With this book, you will be able to carve one of your own! What better way to say "Merry Christmas" to a friend or loved one than with one of these beautiful Santas you carved yourself. It is a timeless Christmas decoration that will be loved for many years to come.

There are a lot of interesting details in this carving, and a lot of opportunities to let your own creativity take over. While most modern Santas are limited to wearing the standard red and white suit, old-world Santas can wear gold, green, blue, purple, and many other colors. His hat can be floppy, pointy, or he could even have a simple hood. His bag is so stuffed with toys that you'll catch yourself peeking in to see if there's anything for you.

As you're getting started, pay close attention to the first steps of the process, preparing the blank for carving. Once the blank is ready, there are so many ways you can go from there. You might want to add more modern elements, like boots and britches, or you might prefer the more traditional look. Take a good look at the gallery for more ideas. Have fun, and merry Christmas!

Carving the Project

For this carving I'm using a piece of basswood that measures 3 1/2" square by 7 1/2" tall. It doesn't matter how tall or thick the block is; it just needs to be square. Begin by drawing a line like this on your wood block.

Use the sawed-off piece to mark the block again on this side.

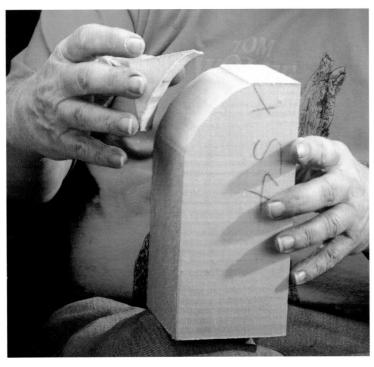

Then saw it off with a bandsaw to look like this.

Then saw it off. The block should look like this.

Measure an inch in on this side.

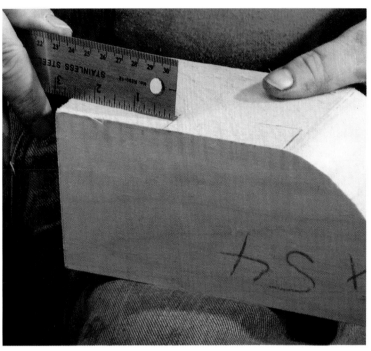

Do the same thing on the other side.

Then measure about two inches up on the same side.

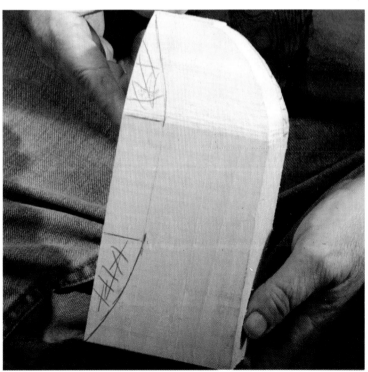

Mark the block like this on both sides.

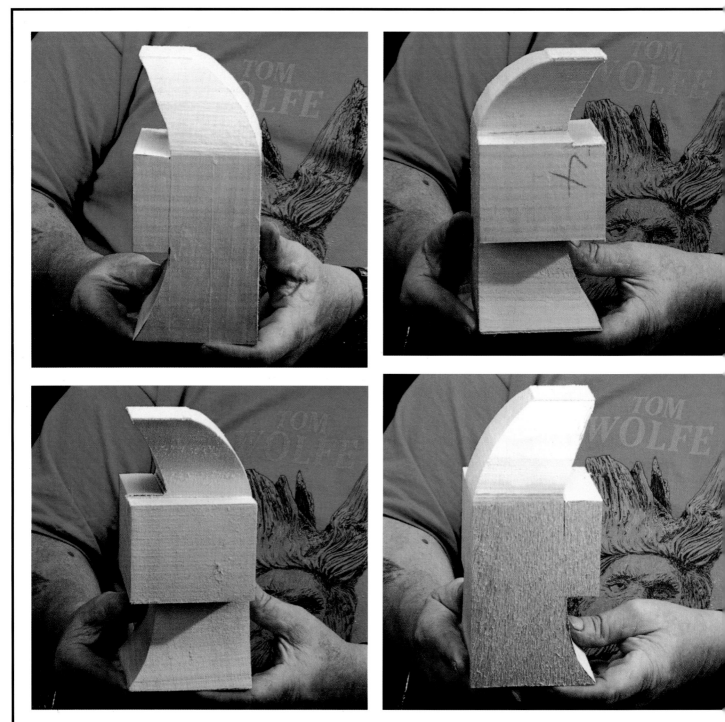

Then cut away the marked pieces so your block looks like this.

Now we need to do some drilling. The square part will be Santa's pack. First measure in 3/4" inch.

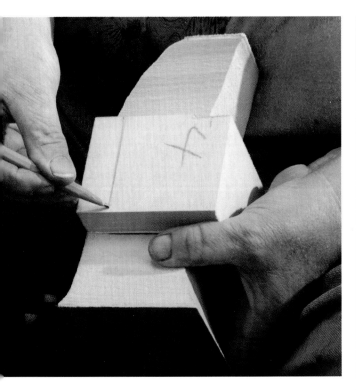

Then draw in a line like this.

This is the part that needs to be drilled (or carved) off. I like to use a Forstner bit.

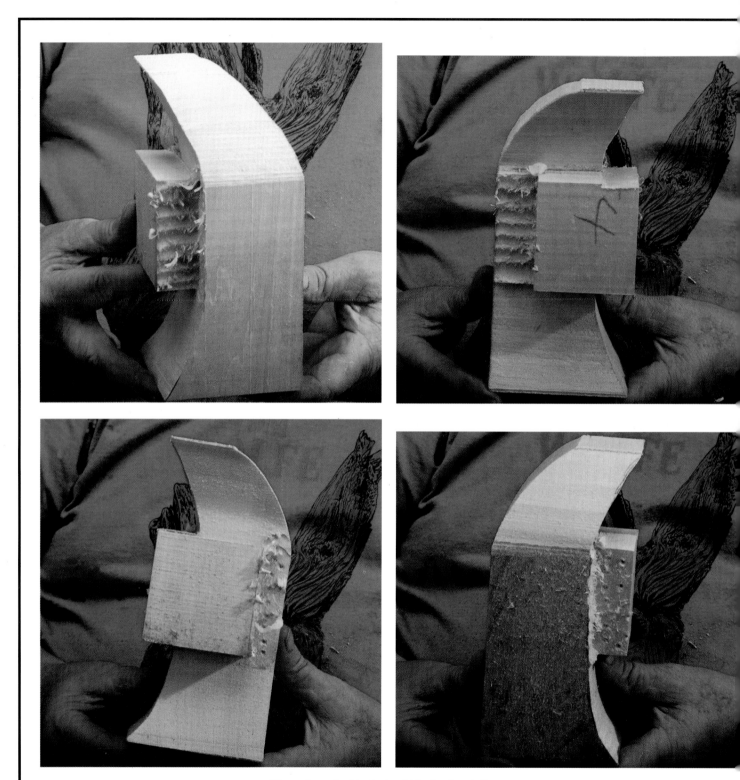

This is how the block should look after drilling.

I'm spraying the block generously with a half-and-half solution of rubbing alcohol and water. The water allows for smoother carving, and the alcohol helps it dry more quickly.

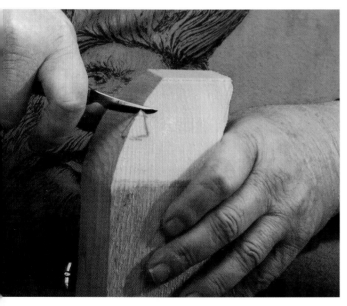

Now we're ready to carve. The first thing we'll do is the nose. Mark a nose something like this and then make a two-cut notch where the bridge of the nose will be.

Then make a stop cut at the bottom of the nose.

Cut up to the stop cut with the knife.

Keep cutting wood away until the nose is as far from the face as you want.

9

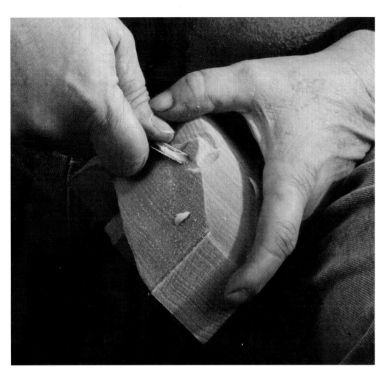

Scoop wood away from the sides of the nose with a gouge.

Cut away the lower corners of the triangle to make room for the nostrils.

Pull away some wood to make an indentation around the nostril (where the smile lines begin) by making three cuts. Do the same on both sides.

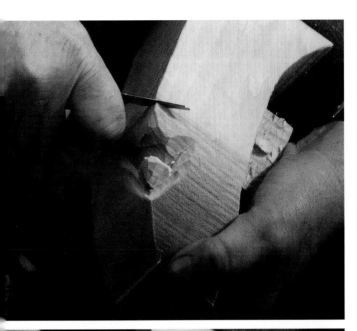

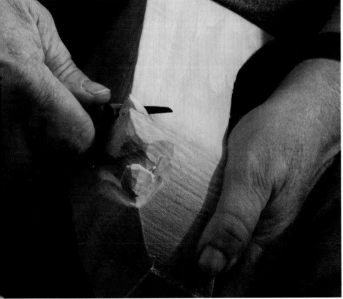

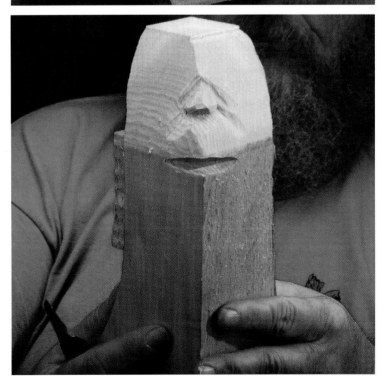

Make a stop cut for the chin whiskers and cut back up to it. It should go in almost as far as the nose does.

Progress.

Now I'm carving wood away from the side of the head to leave room for the shoulders.

Smooth out any drill marks.

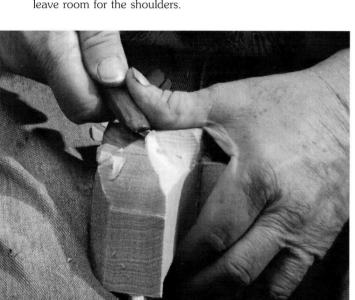

I call this the fulcrum cut. I rest my thumb on the knife handle, and then rock the knife back and forth on it.

Progress. You can see the shoulders beginning to emerge.

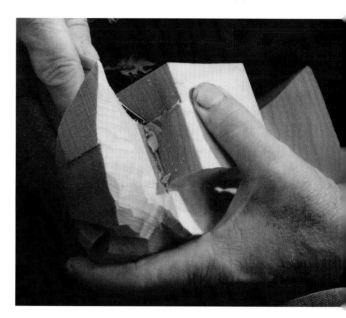

Now I'm going to bring the hood more into the shoulder. Make a stop cut...

...and then cut back to it.

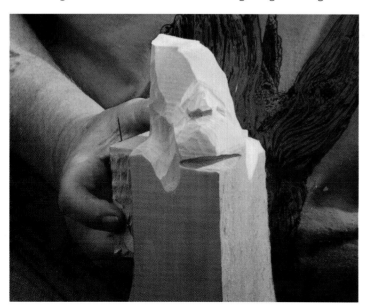

Progress.

A good knife is more flexible, to allow you to get into tight areas with control you wouldn't get from a stiffer knife.

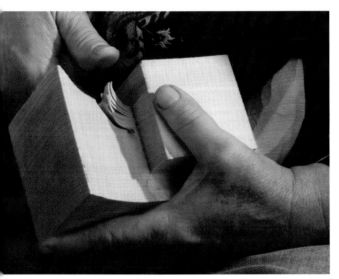

At the bottom of the cloak I'm going to leave a lump for the heel to give more of a walking look. Cut wood away like this...

...and then cut it all off with one cut.

Progress.

For the other foot, which will be poking out of the front of the robe, make a cut at an angle for the top of the foot.

Progress.

Come down from about where the knee should be back to the first cut. Keep making the same two cuts until you pull out enough wood.

I need to narrow the head down to the width it should be. Go back and forth between both sides so you don't carve off too much on one side. Remember he has a hood on, so you're going to want to leave a little extra thickness.

Progress.

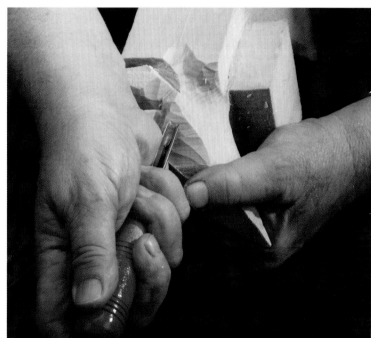

Cut all the way around to mark where the hood meets the face.

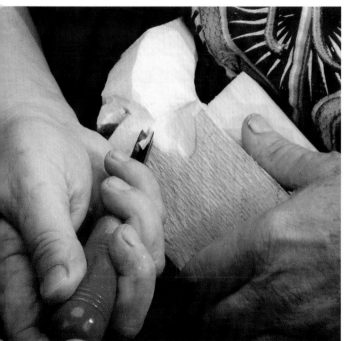

Bring the beard up around the face with the V-tool.

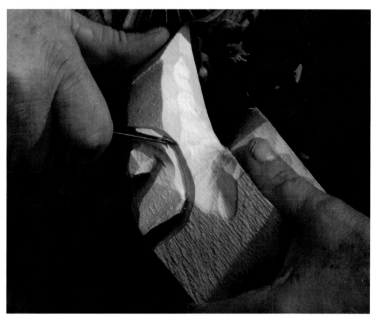

Cut up from the face to the hood with the knife to make the hood look draped around the face.

Progress.

Keep making deeper cuts.

I've marked where the knee and the bottom of the belly belongs. Make a stop cut down by rocking the knife back and forth.

Progress.

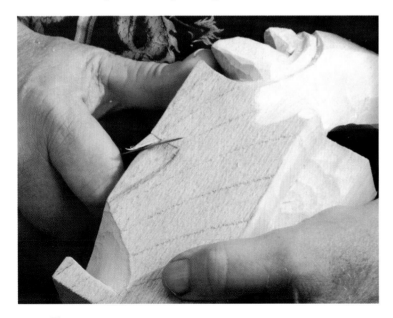

Then cut up to it.

16

Knock off the corners at the bottom on either side. The only part that needs to flare out is the tail of the cloak that drags behind the Santa.

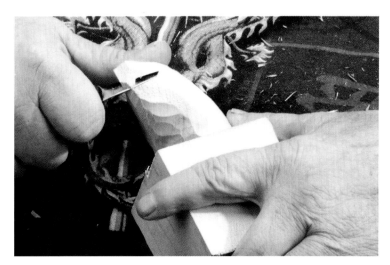

Now I'm taking off the point on the hood.

Progress. Keep it symmetrical by looking at the bottom like this.

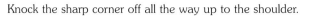

Knock the sharp corner off all the way up to the shoulder.

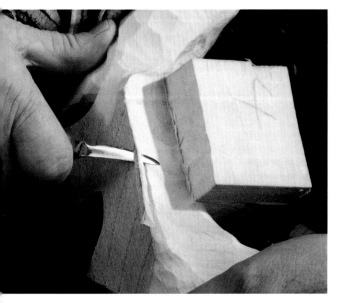

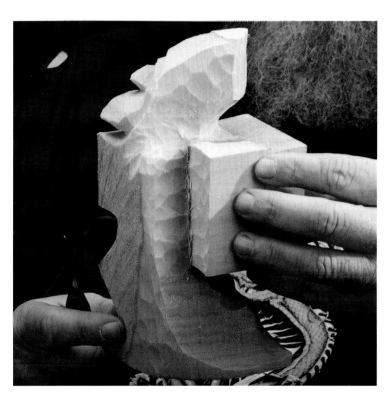

Progress.

Mark out the sack like this.

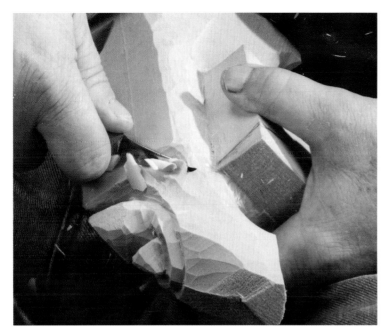

Define the shoulders some more. I want the sack to come over both shoulders like a large knapsack.

I like to carve toys sticking out of the sack. This will be a teddy bear.

First scoop out some wood in a downward direction to define the forehead and muzzle.

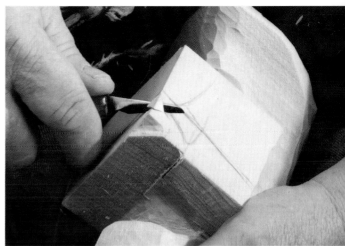

Then make a two-cut notch like this to bring the chin away from the body.

I'm carving wood away from the sides of the face to bring the muzzle out more.

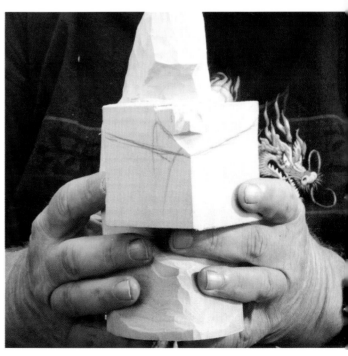

The face is taking shape.

18

Scoop out more wood from underneath the chin, and then square off the muzzle.

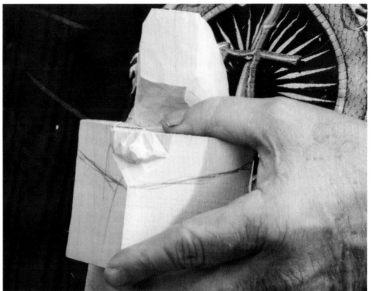

Progress.

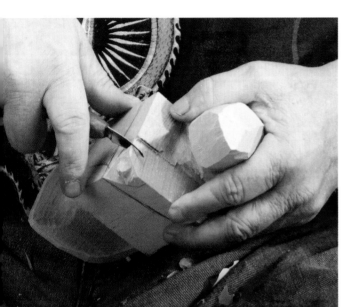

Make a stop cut right in front of the ear...

Bring the ears out with little scoops in an upward direction. You're less likely to break the ear off if you use a V-tool.

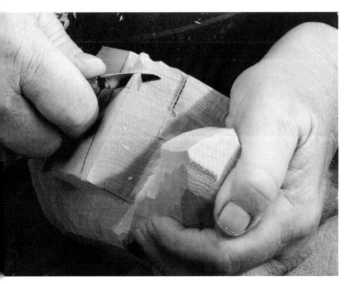

...and then cut up to it from the face.

Progress.

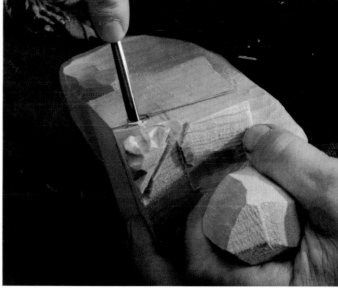

Push straight in with the gouge the whole way around to make a circular stop cut.

I'm marking his paws, which will be coming out over the edge of the bag.

Then use the same gouge to cut towards it from the outside.

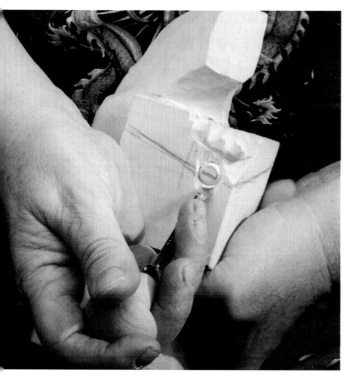

Progress. Do the same thing on the other side.

I'm making an undercut to bring the paws away from the body and to give the appearance that they are coming up out of the bag.

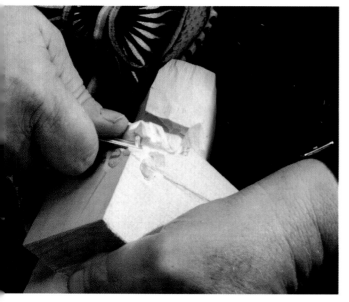

I'm using a veiner to carve more wood out from under the chin.

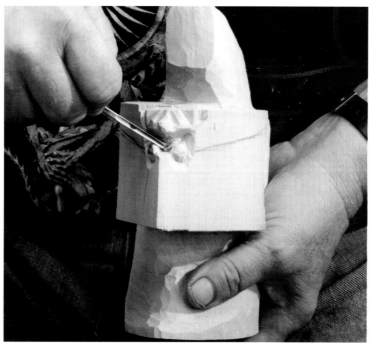

I'm using a small #5 gouge for this tight area. I use it all the time for finer detail work.

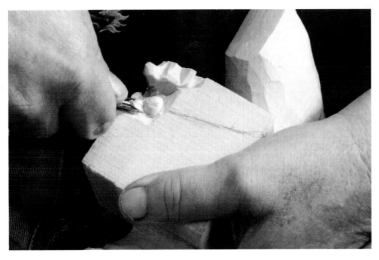

I'm pulling wood from between the paws to establish the top edge of the bag.

Now we'll work on the bag itself. First I'm taking off the sharp corner.

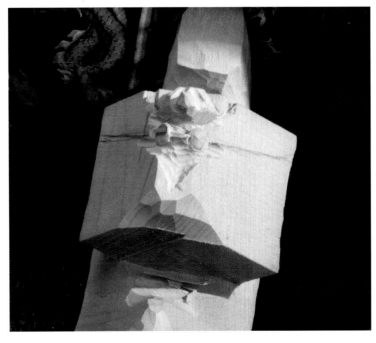

Remember that there's a lot of toys jammed into it, so that means lumps, corners, and odd shapes sticking out.

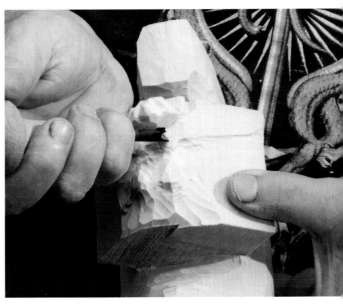

I'm carving out lumps in the bag where the teddy bear's feet are sticking out. Remember to get rid of any pencil marks as soon as you can, because they will both confuse your eye and make your carving dirty.

Progress. Carve out the area behind the ears and round them a little more.

Take a small half-round gouge and scoop a little out between the ey

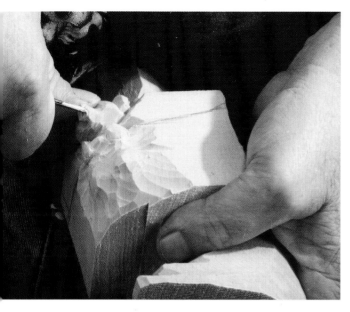

Carving a simple "X" on the muzzle creates the nose and mouth.

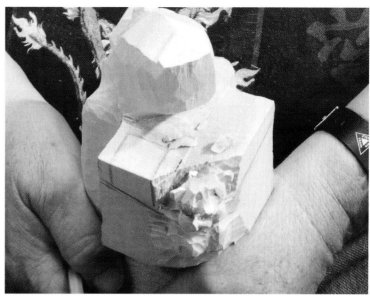

Next I'll carve a box-shaped present, sticking out behind the bear.

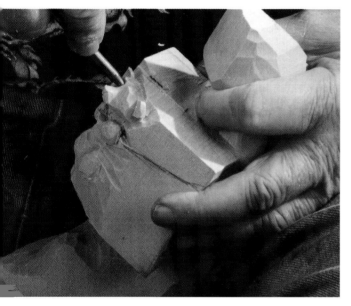

To make the teddy bear's *eyes*, I'm using a small *eye* punch. These punches are my design and they are available from Woodcraft.

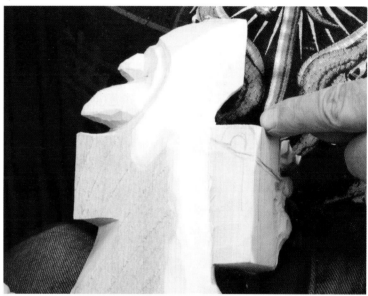

A candy cane would look nice right beside the box.

Progress.

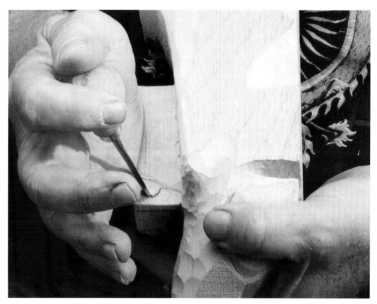

Make a stop cut along the outline of the candy cane with the gouge.

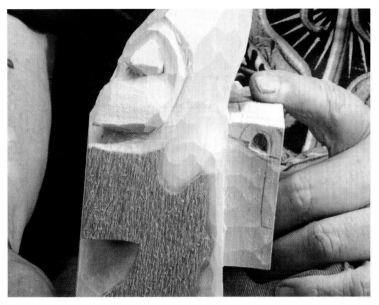

Scoop out the inside of the curve first, and the candy cane will be less likely to break off. Then round the outer edge.

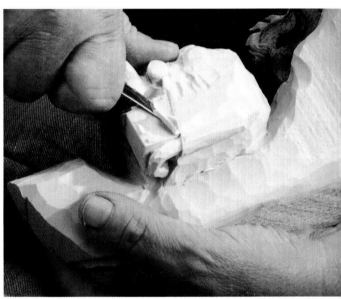

Remember, preserve the lines as they go into the bag.

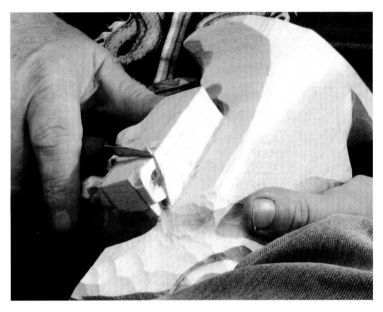

The lip of the bag will come up over the candy cane and box, so carve some wood away from the box, keeping the side nice and smooth.

Progress.

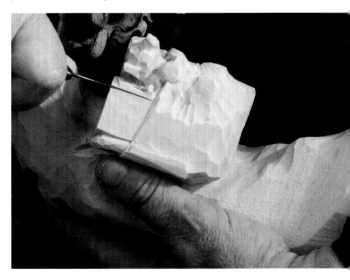

The box needs to be shaped a little more so it looks more like it's jammed in the bag.

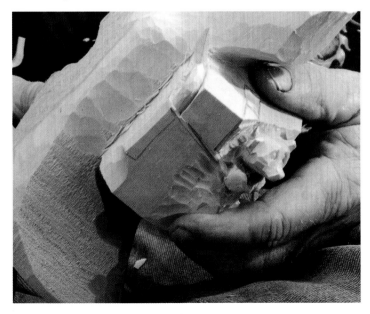

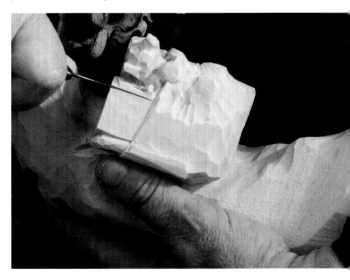

I'm making a deep cut to square off the box and bring it away from the teddy bear.

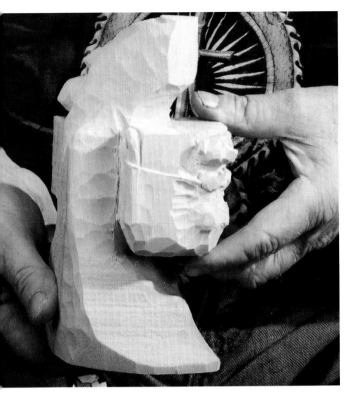

Progress.

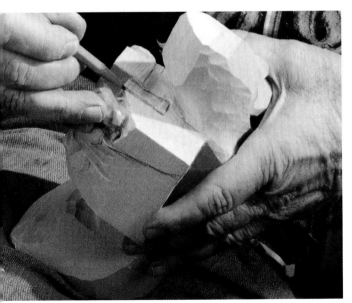

The next thing we'll add to Santa's sack will be a book.

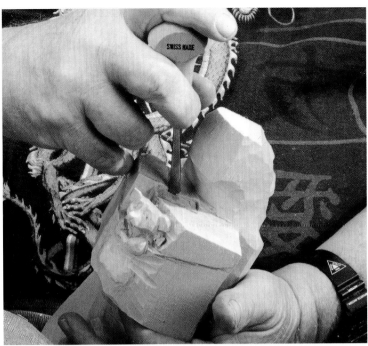

To carve out the book, I'm using the skewer and the flat-end chisel. I don't use either one much at all, but I recommend having them, because when you need them, you need them badly. First I'll use the skewer to make a stop cut on the outline of the book.

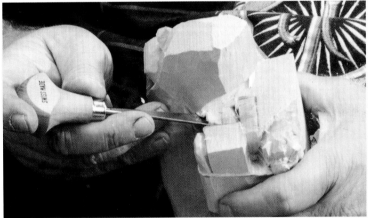

Then I'll cut back to it with the flat-end chisel.

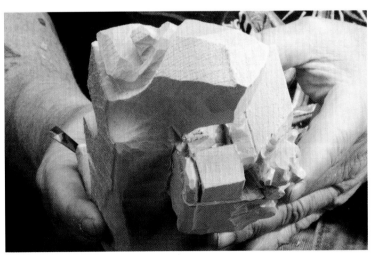

Progress.

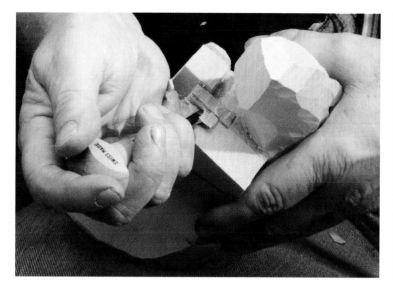

Then use the flat chisel to come at it from the other side.

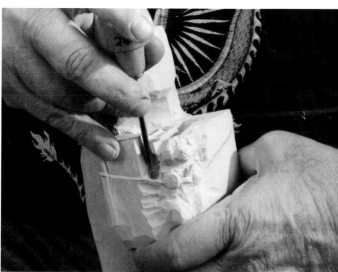

This V-tool is good for making a cut that separates the covers from the pages, as well as the page texture.

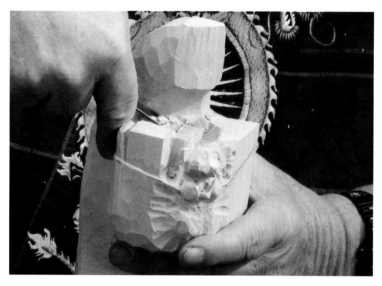

Use your index finger as a depth meter, because if the blade slips, then it won't go further.

Progress.

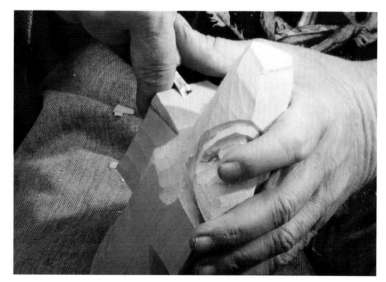

It's also a good idea to rest your other thumb on top of your carving thumb to provide extra counter pressure in case the blade slips.

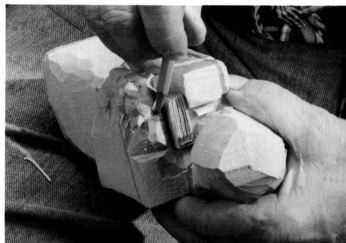

I'd like to put a round wrapped package in behind the teddy bear. I need to scoop this wood out.

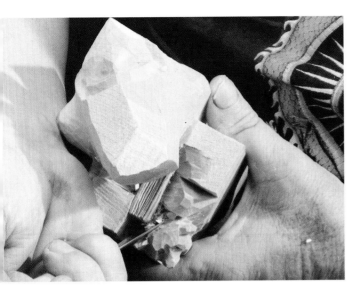

I'm using the skewer to make stop cuts and the flat-end chisel to pull the wood out. Be careful not to carve in to the book.

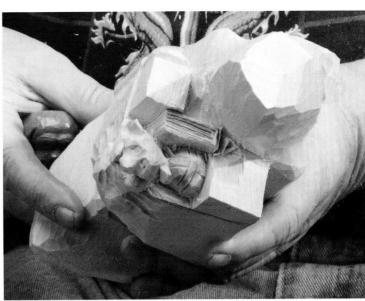

Progress.

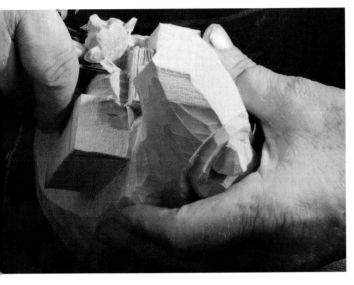

Round the top of the present.

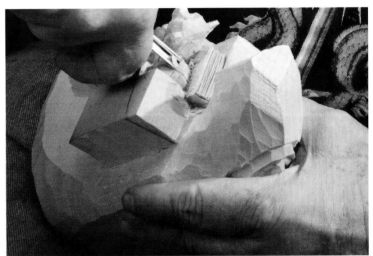

The gouge will make a little gully to make the ribbon look like it's pulled tight.

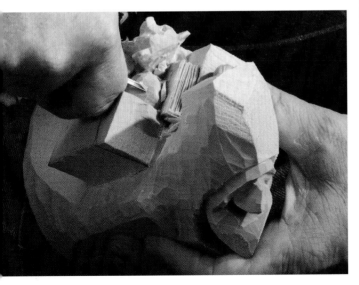

I'm using the small V-tool to carve in ribbon.

The package is finished.

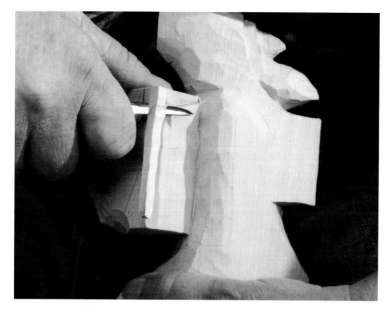

Knock off the other sharp corner on the bag.

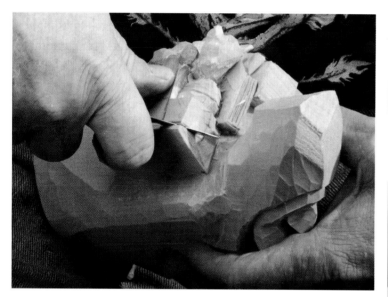

I'm going to add a couple of packages to finish up with the toys in the bag. Start with stop cuts at the edges of the packages.

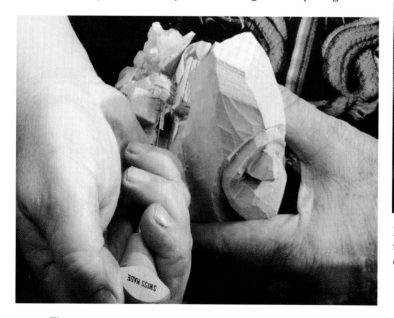

Then scoop away wood from around them.

Progress. Remember that the packages should be different sizes. If things line up too well in the bag, it won't have that "stuffed" look.

I'm finished with the toys in the bag for now. Now we'll work on the bag itself. I'm going to continue the lines on the toys we just carved, like the corners on the boxes and that sort of thing.

28

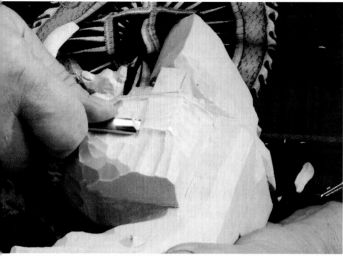

Progress.

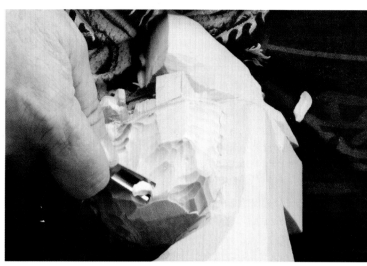

Progress.

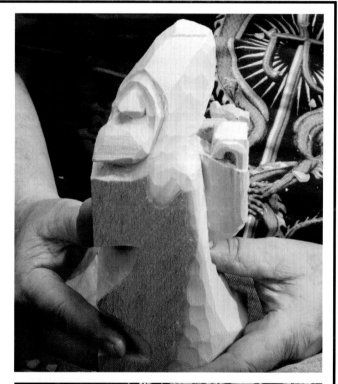

Progress.

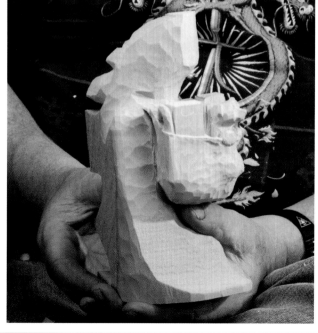

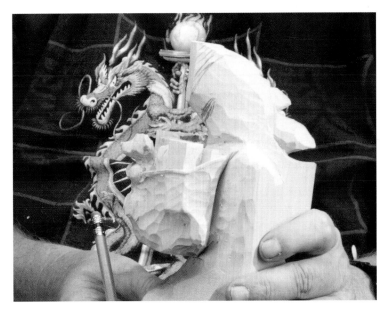

I've decided our Santa will have a tall hat that's drooped over, maybe with a tassle on the end.

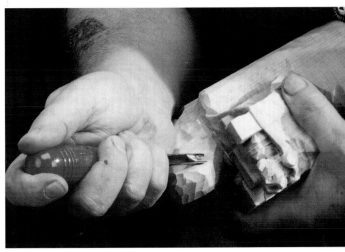

Cut with the V-tool along where the hat folds over. Remember that the hat tapers toward the top.

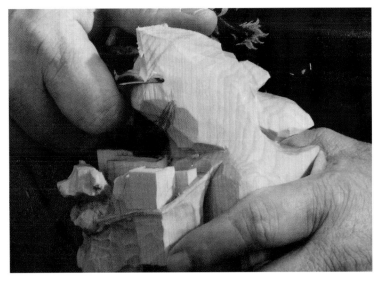

Cut the excess wood off of the top. I sprayed it with the alcohol solution first for easier carving.

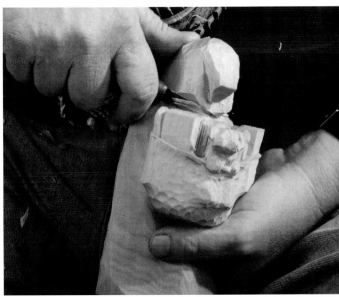

Define the back of the head and the hood by making double cuts. First cut down toward the shoulders...

Progress. Round and shape the head.

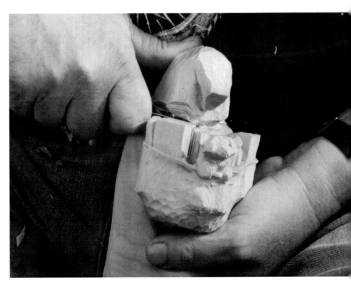

...And back up to get rid of the wood. Do this the whole way around.

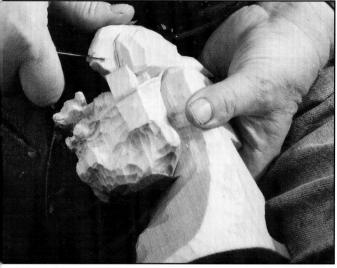

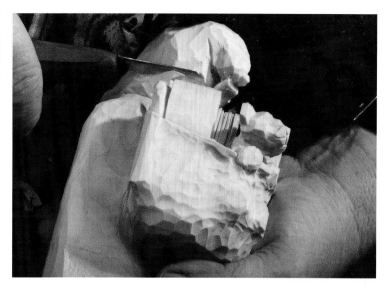

Use the knife to take wood away from the area around the hat.

Use the same kind of cuts (only smaller) to make the tassle.

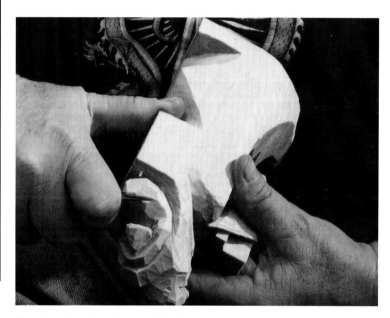

Now I'm trimming the beard back.

Progress.

Cut the foot to size with two cuts. First make a stop cut on the outer edge of the foot...

Then make a cut into it to get rid of the excess.

Progress.

The bottom edge of this box needs to stick out a little more through the bag. I'm using the flat gouge.

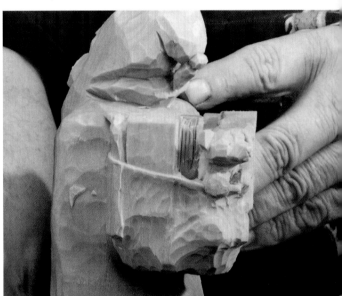

Progress.

The shoulders are too square. I'll narrow them, starting from where the elbows will be, and moving up.

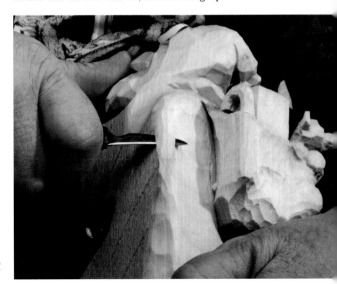

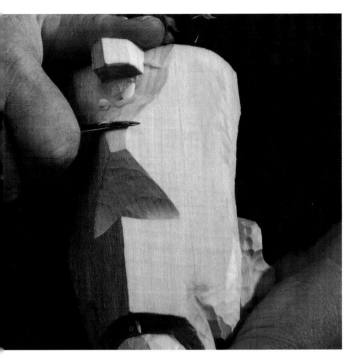

Now we'll do some work on his leg. Square off the point where the knee will be.

I'll change over to the #7 gouge, which is working better than the knife was.

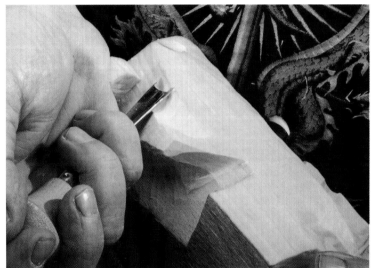

Take some wood away from the other side of the leg, too.

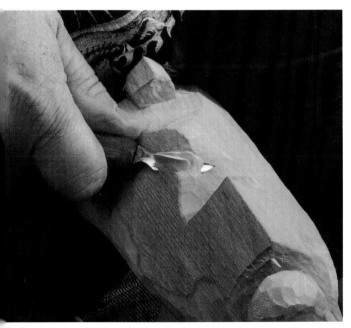

The leg he has forward is his right leg, so I'll carve out a groove on this side of the leg, so the joints are in alignment with the hip.

Progress. At this point, I could keep him as an old world Santa with the robe, or I could pull the robe back and give him britches for a more contemporary look.

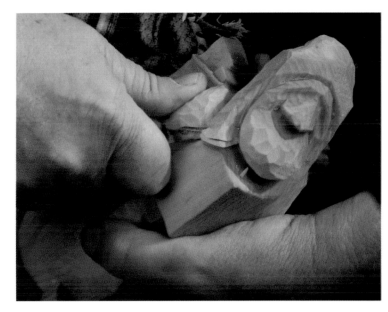

I'm pulling wood from here to start defining the drapery of the robe.

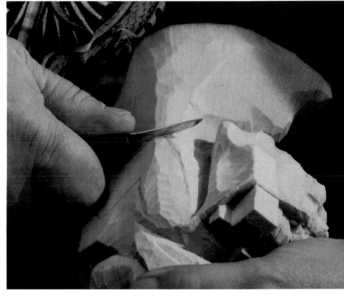

Make a stop cut at the elbow.

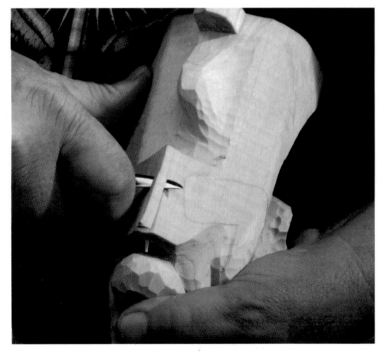

We can also start work on the arms and hands. I have marked where the arms will go, and now I'll smooth out this sharp edge.

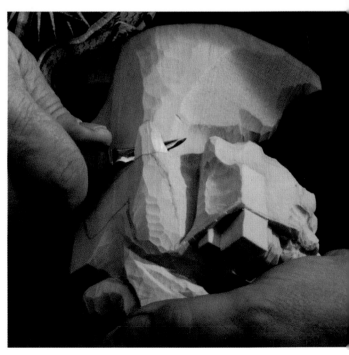

Then cut up to it to bring the arm out.

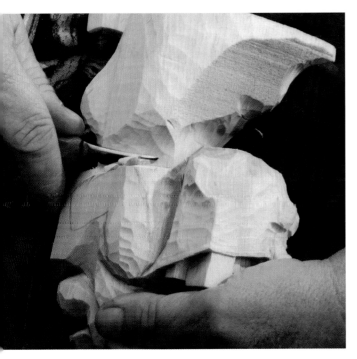

Progress.

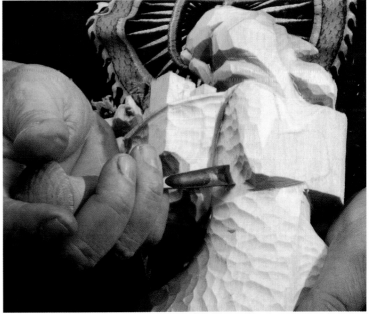

Progress. Pull wood out from behind the upper arm, too.

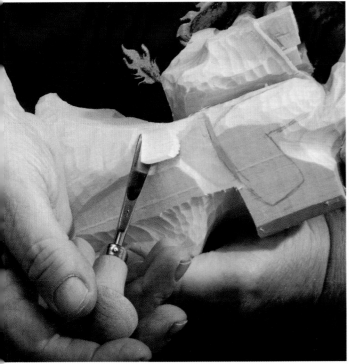

You'll need to take wood out from the hem of the robe all the way up to the elbow. A gouge like this will move a lot of wood faster than a knife can.

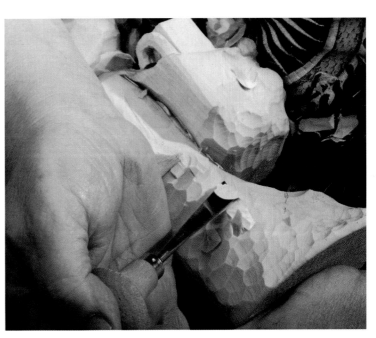

Do the same thing on both sides.

Progress.

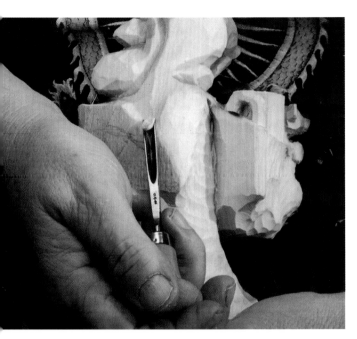

Now we will define the inside parts of the arms. Start with the gouge to establish the crook of the arm.

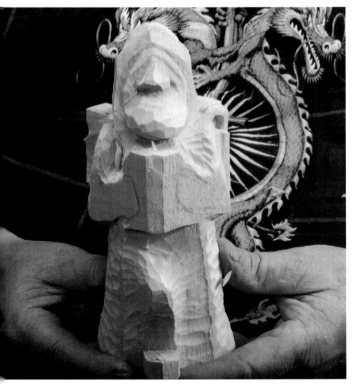

Progress.

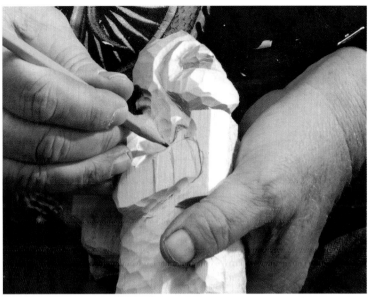

Pull wood away from around the hands. Leave a lump and mark it for the thumb.

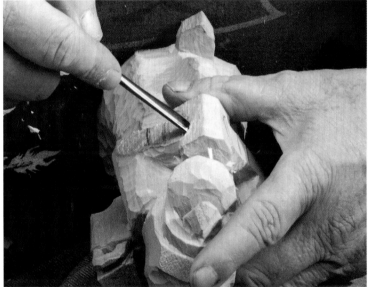

Make a stop cut on the outline of the mitten using the flat gouge.

Then use the knife to remove wood from the surrounding area.

37

Progress.

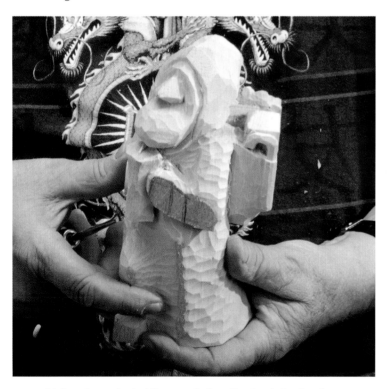

He's going to be holding a rolled up list that he's already checked twice.

To make the paper look rolled up, I'm making a spiral cut with a veiner on each end.

Progress.

For the fur trim on the cuff, make a stop cut...

...And then cut back to it from the mitten.

Progress. Do the same on the other hand.

Progress.

Three double cuts make a crow's foot pattern to show the fabric folds in the crook of the arm.

Progress.

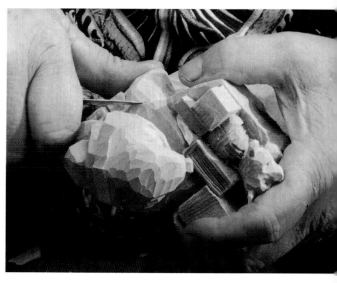

To define the shoulder straps on the bag, make a stop cut along the strapline, over the shoulder and under the arm.

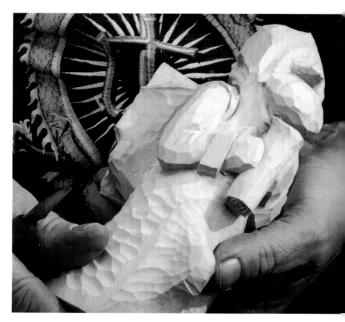

Then cut back to it to make it stand out from the arm.

Continue the strap line under the arm back onto the bag, first making stop cuts.

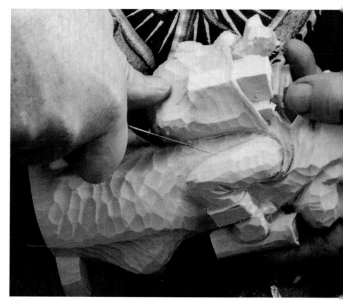

Then cut in towards the stop cuts.

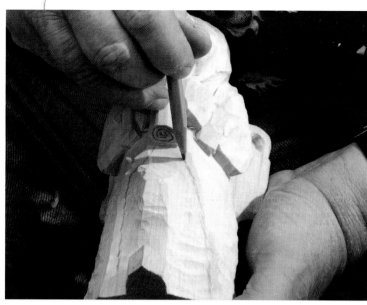

I'm marking in where the edges of the robe will fall.

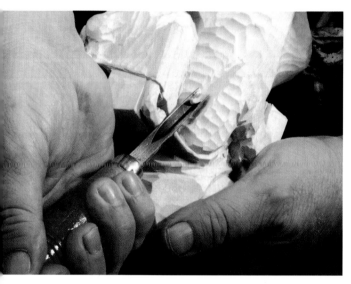

Run the V-tool down the rear edge of the arm to bring it away from the body and give it a more rounded look.

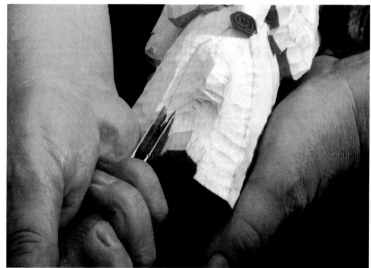

Now I'm using the V-tool to make a cut along the lines I just drew.

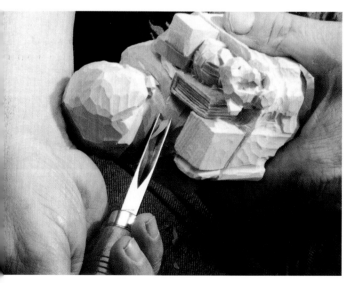

The bag needs to stand out a little bit more from the back and shoulders. I'm making the initial cut with the V-tool and then going in to clean things up with the #9 gouge.

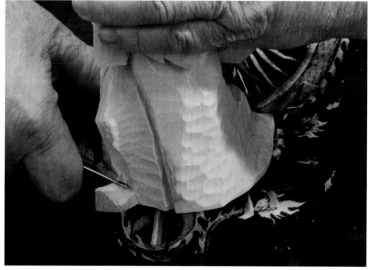

Take some wood off the top of the foot to make an upturned toe.

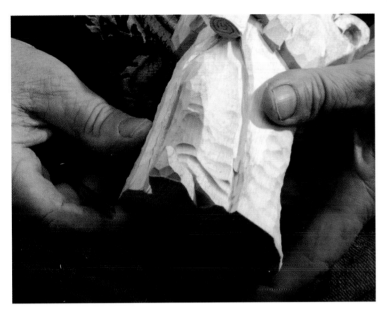

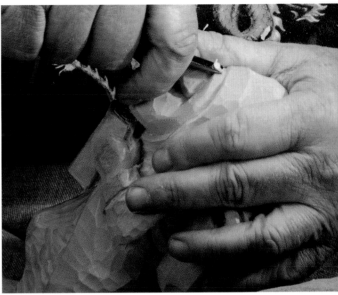

Now we'll go back to work on the face. Separate the eyebrows with the half round gouge.

I've decided to give him the old-world look and give him a long garment under the robe instead of the more modern britches and boots. The fabric needs to fall around the shoe, so I'll add some fold lines with the half-round gouge.

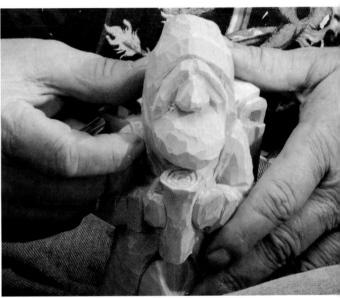

Progress.

Remember the fabric for this garment is much lighter weight, which lets it fold and drape more freely.

Then we'll move on to the nose. Push a half-round gouge straight up the nose to form the nostril.

42

To make the nostril look flared, start with the half-round gouge at the tip of the nose and move in an arc toward the face.

The nose isn't buttony enough, so I'm scooping a little wood from the upper part of the nose.

The new profile.

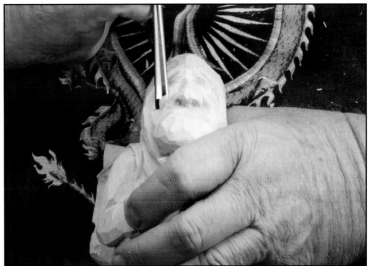

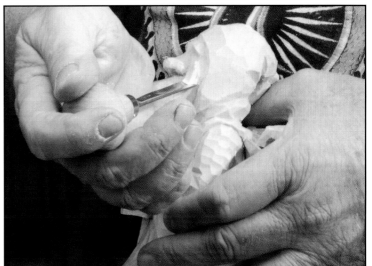

Round the cheeks to make room for a cheery upturned moustache.

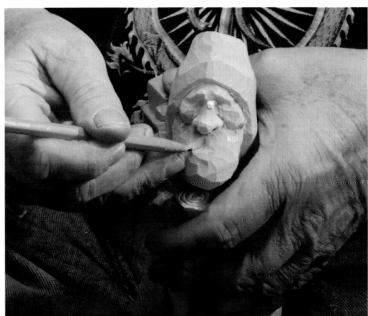

Draw a center line down from between the nostrils, and a line in either direction to mark where the moustache will be. The darkened triangle area is what needs to be removed.

43

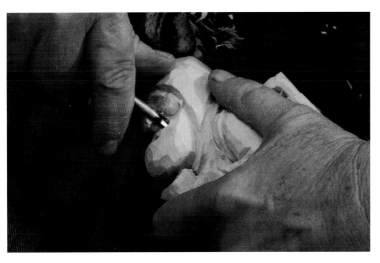

Make a curving stop cut along the moustache line.

Then cut up to it to bring that moustache out.

Progress.

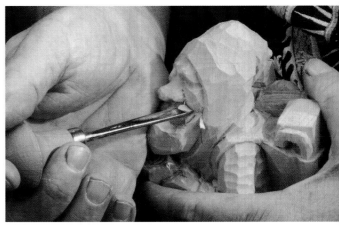

To get the inside curl of the moustache, push the half round gouge into the face on the upper line of the moustache.

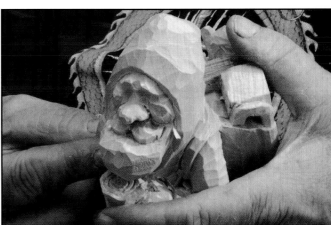

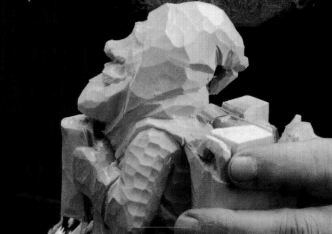

44   Progress.

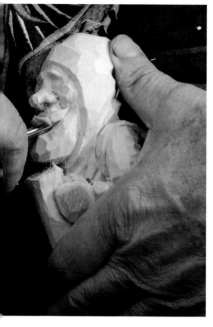

Now for the lip. Use the half-round gouge to start at the center and curve up to the moustache in each direction.

The finished lip.

Progress. The robe will be trimmed in fur like I have marked here.

Cut along the outline for the trim with the V-tool.

Now I'm going back in to clean up the carving, getting rid of gouge and knife marks or anything else that doesn't belong there.

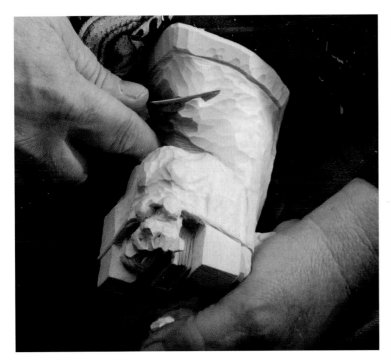

The bulge for the other heel is too large, so I need to cut it down a bit.

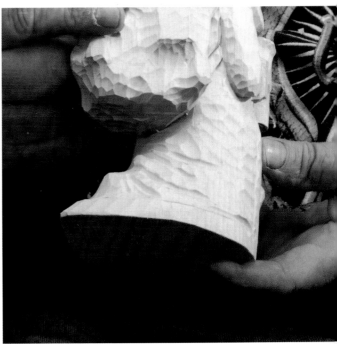

Progress. While I was at it, I added some more fold lines to the robe.

Progress.

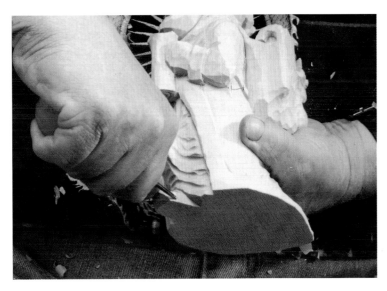

Using the veiner, cut around the bottom of the shoe to make the sole.

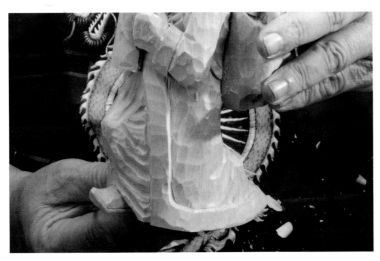

The finished shoe.

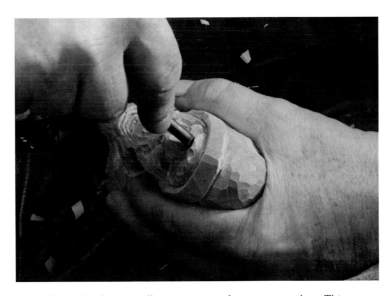

To make the eyes, I'm using one of my eye punches. This one was ground to form a half circle to give a more sleepy or sorrowful look.

The punched eyes.

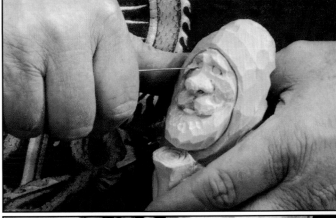

Now carve wedges out to form the corners, using three little cuts.

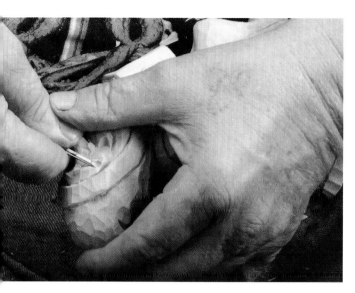

Use the same tool to make hair lines on the hat tassle.

Then take a small V-tool and trace around the edges of the eye to form eyelids.

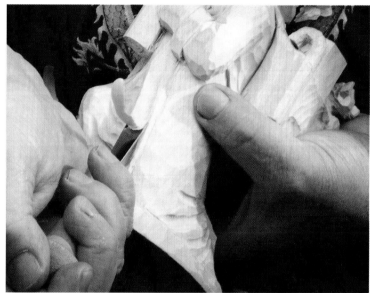

I'm running the gouge along the trim to give it a more concave look and set it apart from the rest of the robe.

A smaller punch forms the irises in the eye.

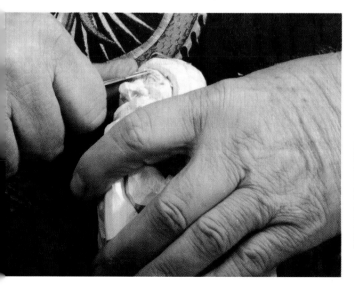

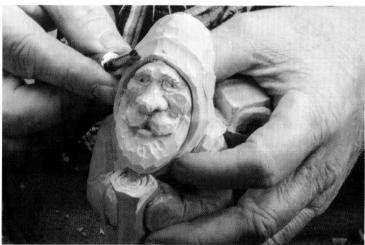

This is a fun tool I made from a leather punch. It's ground flat on one side and has two 45-degree beveled edges. I call it the detail designer.

Use the small V-tool to make hair lines for the eyebrows.

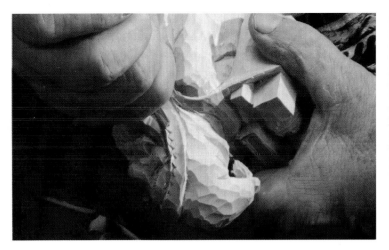

It's great for making all kinds of textures.

The finished carving.

Painting & Finishing the Project

Before I paint the carving, I like to brush on a coat of boiled linseed oil. This allows the paint to go on more smoothly and makes a nice seal for the wood.

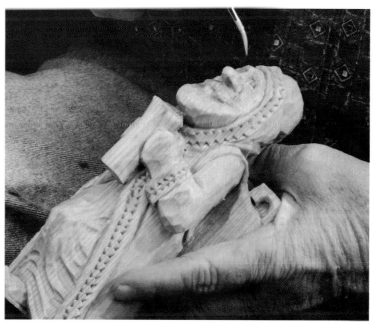

Now we're ready to paint the carving. I like to use artist's oil paints, thinned with turpentine into a stain. That way the wood can still show through.

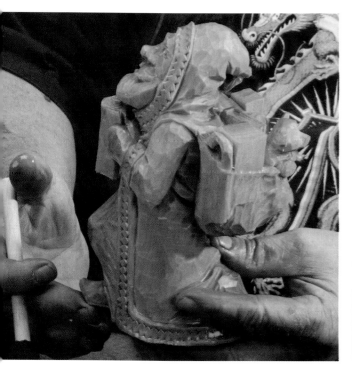

If you can, let it dry overnight. If you're in a hurry, brush on the oil, let it stand for a couple of minutes, and then wipe off any excess with a dry paper towel.

I mix my own shade for flesh, using a touch of flesh color, with a lot of white, and a little raw sienna.

For the blush tones on the cheeks, nose, and lip, I dot on some red.

Progress.

Then blend it in.

This package will also be blue.

I'm using blue mixed with a little violet for the trim on the robe. I like to add many different colors to the trim on these Santas.

The robe, of course, will be red. I'm using Alizarin Crimson.

52

I'm blending some blue over the red for this package for more of a maroon color.

Progress. I don't really like that purple color, so I'm going to paint over it.

I mixed the crimson and the blue with some white for the undergarment. This shade ties the red and the blue on the robe together.

I went back over it with the Vermillion.

53

Some burnt sienna will look nice on the teddy bear.

A little white will bring that tassle right out.

To deepen the shadows a little more, I'm going into the recesses with the burnt sienna.

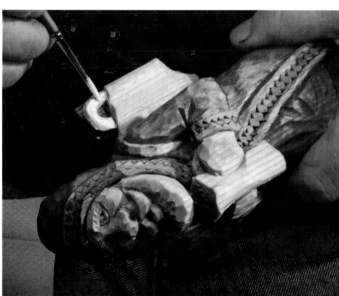

Paint the candy cane with a base coat of white.

This present will be green.

Along with the pages of the book.

The eyebrows and beard are also white...

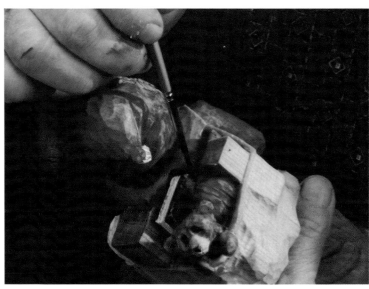

I'll also use black for the book cover and the mittens.

...and so is the list.

Now I'm adding a little white to the corners of the eyes.

Dot on some black for Teddy's eyes and nose.

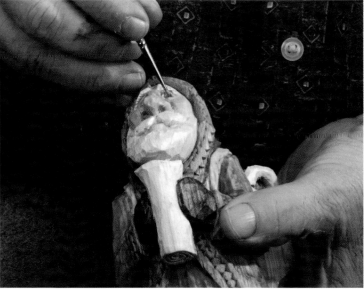

Then I'll dot in some blue for the irises. Now the painting is done, and I'll spray the carving with Deft spray, which fixes the paint and helps it to dry. I still have a couple small details left to paint.

A fine point black marker is handy for small details like the pupils of his eyes.

Use the black marker to put names on the list.

This metallic gold paint is nice for details like the top of the tassle...

The candy cane needs some red stripes.

...and the ribbons on the packages.

The finished carving.

Gallery

62